CW01261186

Original title:
The Harmony of Hearts

Copyright © 2024 Swan Charm
All rights reserved.

Author: Liina Liblikas
ISBN HARDBACK: 978-9916-86-920-8
ISBN PAPERBACK: 978-9916-86-921-5
ISBN EBOOK: 978-9916-86-922-2

Vibration of Love

In whispers soft, our hearts collide,
A dance of souls, where dreams reside.
With every touch, the world ignites,
A melody that feels so right.

Through shadows deep, our light will shine,
A bond unbreakable, yours and mine.
In laughter shared, in tears we bind,
A symphony where love's aligned.

Blossoms of Belonging

In gardens rich where dreams take root,
We find our place, our tender fruit.
Each petal soft, a story told,
In vibrant hues, our hearts unfold.

Together we weave a tapestry bright,
With threads of joy that feel so right.
In every bloom, a promise grows,
In every breeze, our solace flows.

Heartstrings Aligned

With every beat, our hearts conspire,
A fusion deep, a burning fire.
In silence shared, our spirits soar,
An echo found on love's own shore.

Through moments sweet, through trials faced,
With every glance, our love embraced.
In harmony, our souls take flight,
In heartstrings pulled, we find the light.

A Symphony of Together

In rhythms soft, we blend as one,
A melody beneath the sun.
In every laugh, in every sigh,
Together we reach for the sky.

With gentle hands, we carve our way,
In every dusk, in every day.
The world may change, but here we stand,
A symphony, perfectly planned.

Chorus of Kindness

In whispers soft, kindness grows,
A gentle touch, as sunlight shows.
With open hearts, we share our ways,
In this sweet symphony, love plays.

With every word, a warmth we find,
In moments shared, two souls aligned.
Together we rise, through laughter and tears,
The chorus of kindness transcends all fears.

Imprints of Companionship

In quiet hours, our stories blend,
Footprints linger where paths extend.
Each laugh a treasure, each sigh a peace,
In bonds unbroken, love's sweet release.

With every heartbeat, memories thrive,
In the embrace, our spirits arrive.
When shadows fall, we stand as one,
With imprints of joy, our journey's begun.

Undercurrents of Affection

Beneath the surface, feelings flow,
Like rivers hidden, they softly glow.
In glances shared, our truths emerge,
A silent pact, an unspoken urge.

Through storms we sail, in calm we trust,
In every heartbeat, in every gust.
The undulations of hearts entwined,
In depth of affection, we seek and find.

Twilight of Mutual Dreams

As day surrenders to twilight's hue,
In visions shared, our hopes renew.
Together we wander, hand in hand,
Through landscapes painted by future's strand.

In whispered dreams, we carve our fate,
Each thought a star, as we navigate.
In twilight's glow, our spirits soar,
In mutual dreams, we yearn for more.

Notes of Empathy

In quiet whispers, hearts will bloom,
A gentle touch, dispelling gloom.
We rise together, hand in hand,
Embracing warmth across the land.

With every tear, a story flows,
Each burden shared, compassion grows.
Through storms we walk, side by side,
In shadows deep, our love won't hide.

Seeking solace in each other's eyes,
Finding strength as the sun will rise.
With kindred spirits, we shall stand,
Creating hope, a healing band.

In laughter's echo, joy ignites,
Together weaving starry nights.
With every heartbeat, love's decree,
Empathy binds both you and me.

Heartstrings Interwoven

Threads of gold, they intertwine,
Our stories shared, a sacred sign.
Through trials faced, we stand so tall,
In unity, we will not fall.

With gentle hands, we mend the fray,
Each note of love, a sweet ballet.
Together dancing, hearts will soar,
Creating rhythms to explore.

In quiet moments, silence speaks,
The bond we share, it gently peaks.
With laughter bright, we light the way,
In harmony, we seize the day.

Through every tempest, we will steer,
A beacon bright when paths seem clear.
Bound by trust, forever true,
Our song of life, composed by you.

The Essence of Together

Captured moments, fleeting grace,
In every heart, we find our place.
With open arms, we share the load,
Together walking down this road.

Through twilight's glow, we carve our dreams,
With every laugh, a river gleams.
With whispered hopes, we bravely dare,
In unity, we breathe the air.

In every challenge, side by side,
We summon courage, hearts our guide.
In shared reflection, visions grow,
The essence blooms in love's soft glow.

With gratitude, we chart the skies,
In golden hues, our spirits rise.
With joy, we'll write this tale anew,
For life's true essence lies in you.

Bound by Radiance

In light's embrace, we find our way,
Illuminated through each day.
With all our colors, vibrant and bright,
We weave a pattern, pure delight.

Through gentle beams, our spirits dance,
In every moment, we take a chance.
Together shining, hand in hand,
Creating magic as we stand.

With kindness painted on our hearts,
We mend the world with loving parts.
The brilliance shared makes shadows flee,
Forever bound, sweet harmony.

In every heartbeat, brilliance flows,
A shared connection, love bestows.
In twilight's glow, we find our grace,
Bound by radiance, we embrace.

Harmonizing in Silence

In the quiet glow of dawn,
Whispers dance upon the breeze.
Two hearts locked in sweet repose,
Silence speaks where love agrees.

Eyes become the words unsaid,
In stillness, we find our way.
Hands entwined with gentle grace,
Our souls blend where dreams convey.

Every sigh a song unchained,
Softly echoing the night.
In this space, two worlds converge,
Creating magic in the light.

Beat of Mutual Dreams

In the rhythm of the stars,
We chase shadows of our fate.
Each heartbeat, like a drum,
Guides us forth, we resonate.

With every step a promise made,
Together we dance, as one.
Breathless hopes upon the wind,
Chasing rays of morning sun.

Night's embrace, our canvas vast,
Colors blend in twilight's hue.
Together weaving tales of joy,
A tapestry of me and you.

Underneath Shared Canopies

Beneath the branches, hand in hand,
We wander where the wild things grow.
Nature hums a lullaby,
Each leaf a note, in gentle flow.

Dappled light through emerald shades,
Casts our shadows on the ground.
In the hush of sacred woods,
Our secrets shared, by love profound.

Every rustle, whispers low,
Tales of journeys yet to live.
Underneath this leafy home,
With every moment, we forgive.

Journeys of Symbiosis

In the cradle of the earth,
We find pathways intertwined.
Two spirits merging with the soil,
In this dance, our dreams aligned.

Through the winds of time we soar,
Branches reaching for the light.
Together we forge our way,
In every dawn, a shared delight.

As the rivers carve their tales,
So do we etch our own mark.
Unity in every stride,
In this symbiosis, we embark.

Weaving the Infinite

Threads of time intertwine,
A tapestry of dreams,
In whispers soft and fine,
Their essence gently gleams.

Stars above, ever bright,
Guide us through the night,
In echoes of our hearts,
We find our way, our light.

Colors blend, hearts align,
As seasons start to change,
In every pulse, we shine,
Embracing the exchange.

Through valleys, through the skies,
Connections grow and thrum,
No distance can deny,
The songs we make, a hum.

In every stitch, a tale,
Of love and loss and growth,
Together we prevail,
In this vastness, our oath.

Convergence of Sentiments

Hearts collide in silence,
Like rivers seeking seas,
A dance of sweet defiance,
Beneath the swaying trees.

Whispers shared like secrets,
In twilight's soft embrace,
Every gaze reflects,
The warmth of a shared place.

Moments blend and linger,
As shadows softly play,
Each heartbeat, a singer,
Of what words cannot say.

Together, we create,
A symphony of trust,
In every twist of fate,
Love rises, pure and just.

In convergence, we find,
The threads that bind our souls,
In harmony, entwined,
Completion makes us whole.

Constellations of Care

In the night, stars gather,
Whispers of love so bright,
Their glow, like gentle lather,
Cares woven in the light.

Guiding us through shadows,
With stories intertwined,
Through valleys, highs, and meadows,
Hearts forever aligned.

A galaxy of kindness,
In every shimmering spark,
We find strength in the blindness,
Creating joy from dark.

Stardust falls like blessings,
As warmth wraps around tight,
In the vastness, we're confessing,
That love ignites our flight.

So here beneath the skies,
Where all our dreams share air,
We see through open eyes,
The constellations of care.

Chasing the Same Moon

Underneath the same moon,
Dreamers whisper their wishes,
In a world that feels strewn,
With hopes and tender kisses.

Nighttime cradles our fears,
Yet stars illuminate paths,
As laughter drowns out tears,
And love forever lasts.

Together we'll venture,
On journeys undefined,
Each step, a new adventure,
In heartbeats intertwined.

Through the stillness, we roam,
On waves of silver light,
Finding warmth of a home,
In shadows and in flight.

So let us chase the same moon,
With dreams held close and dear,
In the night's gentle tune,
We find each other here.

Tapestry of Connection

In the weave of life we stand,
Threads of hearts, hand in hand.
Every color tells a tale,
In the wind, our hopes set sail.

Woven tight, through joy and pain,
Each strand shines through the rain.
Underneath the same vast sky,
In this bond, we learn to fly.

Moments flicker like bright light,
In shadows, we find our might.
Together as we face the storm,
With every heartbeat, love is warm.

Life's design, a beautiful art,
Crafted from the depths of heart.
With every knot, we grow so bold,
Our stories, forever told.

In the tapestry we share,
Every thread shows that we care.
In our fabric, strong and grand,
Together, we forever stand.

Chords of Affection

Underneath the silver moon,
Softly hums a gentle tune.
Hearts entwined in rhythmic beat,
Dancing where our worlds compete.

Strummed by whispers, warm and clear,
Melodies that draw us near.
With each note, our spirits rise,
In harmony, love never lies.

Through the trials, through the tears,
Chords of strength that calm our fears.
In the silence, we still find,
Echoes of a love entwined.

Together, we compose our fate,
In the music, hearts elate.
Every strum, a promise holds,
In this song, our love unfolds.

With every chord, a story plays,
A melody that never fades.
In this symphony of trust,
Together, we are always us.

Symphonic Embrace

In the quiet, we unite,
Breath of morning, pure and bright.
Symphonies of love resound,
In each heartbeat, peace is found.

Strings of laughter fill the air,
Notes of joy, a whispered prayer.
In the rhythm of our days,
Together, we find our ways.

Underneath the stars so vast,
Every moment, meant to last.
With each embrace, our spirits soar,
In this dance, we want for more.

Life's concerto, bold and true,
In its music, me and you.
Each refrain, a treasure sought,
In this love, we're always caught.

Through every chord, our souls align,
In this symphony, love divine.
Together, we create the sound,
In this world, we are spellbound.

Fragile Threads of Togetherness

A gentle touch, a soft embrace,
In the tapestry, we find our place.
Threads entwined, both strong and frail,
Bound by love that cannot fail.

Moments flicker, fragile light,
In the quiet of the night.
With every whisper, fears subside,
In this bond, we safely hide.

Life may fray at edges tight,
Yet our hearts remain alight.
Through the cracks, love finds a way,
In the dance of night and day.

Together, we weather the storm,
In shared warmth, we feel so warm.
Each thread tells a story true,
In this journey, me and you.

In the fabric of our days,
Love is woven in myriad ways.
Though fragile threads may bend and sway,
Together, we shall always stay.

Rhythmic Intertwining

In shadow and light, we dance,
The beat aligns, hearts enhance.
Fingers trace the paths we roam,
Together we create our home.

With every step, our pulses sync,
A melody of thoughts, we think.
Each twist and turn, a story grows,
In harmony, our spirit flows.

Whispers echo through the night,
Guided by the stars, so bright.
The rhythm of life, sweet and clear,
In every heartbeat, you are near.

As the world fades, we remain,
Entwined in joy, free from pain.
This connection, a sacred bond,
In the dance of life, we respond.

Through valleys deep and mountains high,
We'll chart our course, you and I.
The rhythm of love, ever bold,
In our hearts, the tale is told.

Nest of Shared Spirits

In a cozy nook, we find our place,
Wrapped in warmth, a soft embrace.
Two souls merge, a gentle hum,
In this nest, together we come.

Stories shared as twilight gleams,
In quiet moments, we chase dreams.
With every laugh and tender glance,
Love blooms here, a sacred dance.

Through storms that shake, we sing so loud,
Together we rise, unbowed, unbowed.
The world may change, but here we stay,
In our nest, we'll never stray.

With open hearts, the truth revealed,
In silence strong, our fate is sealed.
The bond we share, a sacred thread,
In this haven, our love is spread.

As seasons shift and time drifts by,
In every sigh, we touch the sky.
In this nest of shared delight,
Together, we shine, pure and bright.

Whispering Connections

Softly spoken, words take flight,
In gentle breezes, hearts ignite.
A tale unfolds in hushed refrain,
In whispered truths, we break the chain.

Eyes that meet in secret glance,
In silence shared, we take a chance.
The curling tendrils of our thoughts,
In quiet moments, love is sought.

Each sigh, a bridge that brings us near,
In whispered dreams, we conquer fear.
With every heartbeat, every sigh,
In our connection, we learn to fly.

Through misty paths where shadows play,
Our voices dance, they find their way.
In the echoes of the night we share,
A whisper's touch, a love laid bare.

With every heartbeat, we're entwined,
In the garden of our souls, aligned.
In whispered vows beneath the stars,
Our connection glows, no more scars.

Whispers of Unity

In the quiet, voices merge,
A symphony of souls, we surge.
With every whisper, bonds we weave,
A tapestry of love, believe.

In the silence, hearts resound,
On this journey, we are found.
Each gentle touch, a soothing balm,
Together we create, a calm.

Through the echoes of our dreams,
A unity that softly beams.
In whispered hopes, we touch the light,
Guided by the stars, so bright.

With every breath, we understand,
In unity, we take our stand.
Through storms that rise and rivers flow,
In whispers deep, our spirits glow.

As time unfolds, our paths align,
In the dance of life, divine.
In every whisper, every sigh,
Together, forever, you and I.

Together in Sunrise

In the soft glow of dawn, we stand,
Gentle whispers of the morning breeze.
Hand in hand, we trace the land,
Awakening dreams in the rustling trees.

Golden rays kiss the dewy grass,
Birds sing melodies so sweet.
In this moment, time seems to pass,
Together, our hearts skip a beat.

The sky painted in hues of gold,
Promises made in the quiet light.
Stories of love and life unfold,
A beautiful canvas, a shared sight.

As the sun climbs, shadows retreat,
Every step, a dance of our fate.
In this embrace, the world feels complete,
Together in sunrise, never too late.

We gather warmth in each other's gaze,
As day breaks, our spirits soar high.
In love's embrace, we find our ways,
Together forever, you and I.

Chords of Affection

Life plays a melody soft and sweet,
Each note a whisper, every beat a chance.
In harmony, our hearts will meet,
Dancing together in a timeless dance.

Strumming the strings of fate divine,
Resonating love in the air we share.
With every chord, the stars align,
Creating a symphony beyond compare.

In laughter and tears, we compose,
A song that echoes through the years.
Through highs and lows, our love grows,
In each other's arms, we conquer fears.

In the silence, a rhythm is born,
Filling the void with a tender touch.
In the light of day, or soft twilight worn,
Through chords of affection, we feel so much.

Together we create the perfect tune,
With every heartbeat, our lives entwined.
Underneath the watchful moon,
In the music of love, our souls aligned.

Synchronicity of Souls

In the universe's vast embrace,
Two spirits dance, perfectly in tune.
Bound by fate in a timeless space,
They shine together like stars in June.

Every glance feels like a spark,
Drawing closer through the cosmic night.
In the darkness, they leave a mark,
A bond illuminated by gentle light.

Time may twist and tides may turn,
Yet their paths will always align.
In each heartbeat, the fire will burn,
A synchronicity both rare and divine.

In laughter shared and whispers low,
Life's rhythm flows in sweet refrain.
Through every joy and every sorrow,
Their souls united, they'll never wane.

As the world spins in its endless dance,
They find solace in each other's eyes.
In the paradox of chance, a romance,
Two souls journeying through the skies.

Merging Rhythms

Two hearts beat in a steady flow,
Dancing to the rhythm of the night.
In silent moments, feelings grow,
As stars align with soft silver light.

With every shared laugh and sigh,
A melody builds, sweet and true.
In this harmony, we learn to fly,
Discovering love in shades of blue.

The world fades, leaving echoes behind,
A song of two, woven with care.
In the cadence of thoughts intertwined,
We navigate love with grace, we dare.

Hand in hand, our paths intertwine,
With every heartbeat, the music swells.
Together, we cross the sacred line,
In merging rhythms, our story dwells.

In the depths of night, we take our chance,
To dance to a beat that feels just right.
In every glance, we find our romance,
Merging rhythms under the moonlight.

Moments Shared

In twilight's grace, we find our way,
Two hearts entwined, come what may.
The laughter echoes, soft and clear,
In whispered secrets, we draw near.

Through storms and calm, hand in hand,
Together we rise, together we stand.
The memories bloom, like flowers bright,
Under the canopy of starlit night.

Each glance a promise, each smile a sign,
In this dance of life, you are mine.
With every moment, the world fades away,
In the tapestry of us, forever we stay.

Time may pass, the seasons change,
But in our hearts, we remain strange.
An endless journey, we undertake,
Moments shared, for love's own sake.

Through the Same Lens

In the silent night, we gaze and dream,
Two souls together, a flowing stream.
The stars align, they whisper our names,
In the depths of time, our love remains.

We seek the truth in shadows cast,
Through the same lens, both present and past.
With each spoken word, a bridge we build,
In the fire of trust, our hearts are thrilled.

Moments we cherish, captured in gold,
Stories unfold, and secrets told.
Through laughter's light and sorrow's veil,
Together we journey, through every trail.

In colors vivid, our dreams take flight,
Through the same lens, we ignite the night.
Bound by a vision, so deep, so true,
In this shared moment, it's me and you.

As One in the Cosmos

A cosmic dance in the velvet sky,
With every heartbeat, we learn to fly.
Stars intertwine, like our fates aligned,
In this universe vast, our spirits intertwined.

Galaxies whisper, of journeys ahead,
As one in the cosmos, with dreams widely spread.
Cosmic winds carry our hopes, so bright,
In the arms of eternity, we find our light.

Through every heartbeat, through the decay,
We stitch together the night and day.
In stardust and shadows, we find our place,
As one in the cosmos, an endless embrace.

In waves of creation, we dare to believe,
Each moment alive, so hard to conceive.
Together we'll wander, in worlds to explore,
As one in the cosmos, with so much in store.

Wings of Affinity

With wings of affinity, we take to flight,
In harmony's rhythm, we share the light.
The winds of change whisper our names,
As we soar together, casting new flames.

Through valleys and peaks, we journey on,
In each other's presence, we feel so strong.
Our spirits rise, like eagles in grace,
In the boundless expanse, we find our space.

Colors of friendship paint the skies bright,
With every shared moment, we bask in delight.
In the stillness of dawn or the hush of dusk,
Our wings of affinity, a sacred trust.

Through laughter and tears, we navigate time,
In the symphony of life, we create our rhyme.
Together we'll dance, in the freedom we know,
On wings of affinity, our spirits will grow.

Bridges Across the Heart

In the quiet, paths entwine,
Two souls meet, in heart's design.
Bridges built with whispered dreams,
Together, stronger than it seems.

With every step, a heartbeat shares,
Stories told through lingering stares.
Concrete strength and gentle sighs,
Love's foundation never lies.

Through the storms and sunny days,
Hand in hand, we'll find our ways.
Across the chasm, we will leap,
In unity, our secrets keep.

When shadows cast their fleeting doubt,
We find our voices, scream and shout.
The bridge we build, a work of art,
A testament to every heart.

So let us dance, let love ignite,
Two hearts as one, forever bright.
For every bridge that we will cross,
In love, there's never any loss.

In the Same Frequency

In quiet tones, our laughter sighs,
A melody that never dies.
Waves of comfort, soft and clear,
We find our rhythm, drawing near.

In every glance, a silent cue,
A harmony that feels so true.
Together, drifting on the breeze,
Connected souls that flow with ease.

The pulse of life, a shared refrain,
Through highs and lows, through joy and pain.
In sync we dance, in time we move,
In this embrace, our hearts approve.

When static lingers, doubts take hold,
We tune our hearts, be brave, be bold.
In frequencies that intertwine,
Our spirits soar, our fates align.

So let the world fade, fade away,
In this moment, we will stay.
In the same frequency we'll find,
A bond that echoes, forever kind.

A Tapestry of Moments

Each thread a story, woven tight,
In colors vivid, pure delight.
Moments captured, rich and rare,
A tapestry beyond compare.

Stitched with laughter, edged with tears,
Woven memories through the years.
Every knot a tale to tell,
In this fabric, we've lived well.

With every glance, a memory glows,
As life unfolds, the tapestry grows.
Patterns form from love and loss,
A living quilt that won't gloss.

In the quiet, a stitch takes place,
In bustling life, a gentle grace.
Threads connect, both near and far,
In this weave, we find who we are.

So cherish each moment, hold it tight,
For every thread, a brand new light.
In this tapestry, we belong,
A masterpiece, our love, our song.

Waves of Understanding

In the silence, whispers flow,
Tides of thoughts begin to grow.
Understanding, like the sea,
Waves that come and set us free.

With every pulse, we learn to trust,
In gentle rhythms, fair and just.
Through closeness, barriers fade away,
In the calm, we find our sway.

When storms arise, we stand as one,
Facing hardships 'til they're done.
Rising tides may crash and crash,
But in our hearts, we'll make a splash.

Each ebb brings clarity anew,
In every wave, a bond so true.
With open hearts, we'll ride the flow,
In understanding, ever grow.

So let us dance upon the shore,
In these waves, we'll seek for more.
For in each swell, a chance to see,
The depth of love and unity.

Interconnected Passions

In the dance of vibrant dreams,
Our spirits chase the light,
With every heartbeat shared,
We ignite the endless night.

Through laughter and through tears,
We weave a tapestry bright,
Connected by a thread,
That pulls us through the fight.

In whispers soft and sweet,
Our fears begin to fade,
Each passionate embrace,
A promise swiftly made.

In the glow of starlit skies,
We savor all we are,
Intertwined in this moment,
We're each other's guiding star.

Together we will soar,
Into tomorrows new,
Bound by dreams and visions,
And all that we hold true.

Gardens of Mutual Bloom

In each garden, love does grow,
With petals soft and bright,
Shared laughter in the breeze,
Creates a pure delight.

Our roots entwined beneath,
In earth rich and profound,
We nurture every dream,
Where hope and joy abound.

With every gentle rain,
Our spirits xBloom and rise,
In sunlit afternoons,
We paint the endless skies.

Among the blooming flowers,
We find a sacred space,
Where hearts can freely wander,
And souls can gently trace.

Together we shall thrive,
In gardens lush and true,
Unfurling all our colors,
In every shade anew.

Enchanted Paths

We wander through the forest deep,
Where secrets softly sigh,
The paths we choose converge and meet,
Beneath the boundless sky.

Amidst the ancient trees,
We carve our tales anew,
With every step we take,
The world unfolds for you.

Through dappled light and shadow,
Our footprints intertwine,
Exploring all the wonders,
Of love that's truly divine.

With every whispered promise,
The journey hums along,
Together we create,
An ever-lasting song.

On enchanted paths we tread,
Where magic comes alive,
With each heartbeat echoing,
In the dreams we both strive.

Souls Intertwined

In the quiet of the night,
Our whispers softly blend,
Two souls that dance as one,
Finding love without end.

Through journeys far and wide,
We share our hopes and fears,
A bond that time won't break,
Through laughter and through tears.

With every heartbeat felt,
Our spirits begin to soar,
In the warmth of your embrace,
I find what I adore.

Together side by side,
As stars begin to shine,
We write our sacred story,
In rhythms so divine.

With hands held tightly close,
We face the unknown road,
Two souls forever joined,
Love's everlasting ode.

Whispers of Unison

In twilight's glow, we find our song,
Silent echoes where we belong.
Hearts entwined, as stars align,
The night sings soft in sweet design.

Beneath the moon, our secrets shared,
In tender moments, we are bared.
Laughter dances on the breeze,
In whispered dreams, we find our ease.

Time stands still as we embrace,
A tranquil world, a sacred space.
Melodies drift, both near and far,
Together we shine, a radiant star.

When shadows fall and fears arise,
We lift each other, reach for the skies.
With every note, our spirits soar,
In whispers soft, we seek for more.

In unison, our hearts will blend,
A timeless bond that will not end.
Through every trial, we will stand,
In whispers of love, hand in hand.

Melodies of Connection

In gentle chords, our spirits meet,
The rhythm flows, a steady beat.
Together we hum, a sweet duet,
In harmonies, we won't forget.

Through valleys deep, and mountains high,
Our voices rise, they touch the sky.
In melody, our souls unite,
A spark is born in darkest night.

With every chord, a story told,
Of dreams we chased, both young and old.
We dance between the notes so free,
In every sound, a piece of me.

The music swirls, and time stands still,
A timeless bond that holds a thrill.
In symphonies, our hearts entwine,
In melodies of love divine.

Together we create a song,
In every note, we both belong.
Through life's vast stage, we shall roam,
In melodies, we've found our home.

Echoes in Embrace

In shadows deep, where whispers wane,
Embraces shared, release the pain.
The echoes linger, soft and sweet,
In silence, love finds its beat.

Through every sigh, a breath we take,
In gentle arms, our hearts won't break.
With every pulse, a rhythm flows,
In echoes soft, our passion grows.

The world may spin, but here we stand,
In quietude, we understand.
A sacred space, a vow held tight,
In echoes, we become the light.

In twilight hours, we find our grace,
With every glance, a warm embrace.
Through whispered words, our spirits soar,
In echoes deep, we dream of more.

So hold me close, and never part,
With every beat, you own my heart.
In echoes shared, we are set free,
In timeless love, just you and me.

Threads of Serendipity

In woven paths, our journey starts,
With threads of fate, we share our hearts.
In serendipity, we find our way,
Wrapped in warmth, come what may.

Every twist leads us closer still,
Life's tapestry is crafted with skill.
With colors bright, our dreams unfold,
In laughter shared, our stories told.

Through tangled lines and gentle pulls,
We navigate with hopeful glows.
In every stitch, a love profound,
In threads of joy, we are unbound.

When storms may rise, we'll hold on tight,
With threads of peace, we'll find the light.
In serendipity, we dance as one,
Creating magic 'til day is done.

So take my hand, let's weave our fate,
In threads of love, we celebrate.
With every heartbeat, hopes reside,
In serendipity, stand side by side.

Enchanted Synergy

In twilight's glow, dreams intertwine,
With whispered hopes, our hearts align.
Together we dance, a symphony sweet,
Two souls entwined, destined to meet.

Stars above us, secrets to share,
Silent promises fill the air.
Hand in hand, we wander the night,
Guided by love, our spirits take flight.

Nature's canvas, vibrant and wide,
We paint our journey with joy as our guide.
Through valleys and peaks, we chase the dawn,
In the magic of us, we bloom, we belong.

The rhythm of laughter, a soft, sweet sound,
Echoes of joy in the moments we've found.
In echoes of dreams, we share our song,
Together forever, where we both belong.

In this dance of life, we gently sway,
With every breath, love leads the way.
Enchanted synergy, our heart's decree,
In this timeless bond, just you and me.

Echoing Kindness

In every smile, a gentle spark,
A ripple of warmth, igniting the dark.
Acts of kindness, a soft embrace,
In the depths of sorrow, love finds its place.

Through open hearts, compassion flows,
A garden of hope where kindness grows.
With every word, we weave a thread,
That binds us together, where love is spread.

From stranger to friend, a bridging light,
We share our burdens, our joys ignite.
In moments of silence, our souls entwine,
Echoing kindness, a symphony divine.

Through trials faced, we rise and stand,
Together we forge a stronger band.
In acts so small, yet mighty and bright,
Echoing kindness, our hearts take flight.

Each whisper of care, a beacon to guide,
In every gesture, love will reside.
Let us be the light that brightens the day,
In echoing kindness, we'll find our way.

Embrace of Familiarity

In the warmth of home, where laughter rings,
We share our stories, the joy it brings.
In every glance, a tale we know,
An embrace of familiarity, where love can grow.

With every sunrise, we greet the day,
Finding comfort in the simple way.
With hands held tight, we face the world,
In the embrace of family, our dreams unfurled.

The scent of shared dishes, a savory bite,
In gatherings warm, we feel the light.
Through seasons that change, our roots run deep,
Embrace of familiarity, promises we keep.

In laughter and tears, we share the weight,
Together we navigate love and fate.
With whispers of wisdom, our hearts will soar,
In this sanctuary, we'll always explore.

So let us cherish each moment dear,
In the embrace of familiarity, we conquer fear.
For in this bond, timeless and true,
Love is the language spoken by you.

Strands of Affinity

In the tapestry of life, we weave our tale,
Strands of affinity, where spirits sail.
With colors of passion, threads of gold,
A bond unbroken, a story retold.

Through gentle whispers, we share our dreams,
In every heartbeat, a promise gleams.
Together we rise, through storm and sun,
Strands of affinity, forever as one.

Each laugh a note, in our song of grace,
In this woven pattern, we find our place.
With every embrace, a love so rare,
Strands of affinity, a precious care.

As seasons shift, and shadows fall,
We stand united, we conquer all.
In the dance of time, our spirits entwined,
Strands of affinity, forever aligned.

So let us cherish this bond we share,
Through trials and triumphs, everywhere.
In this beautiful weave, so endlessly bright,
Strands of affinity guide us to light.

Luminescent Connections

In the quiet night, lights glow,
Whispers of hope begin to flow.
Across the distance, hearts entwine,
A tapestry of souls align.

Stars above like dreams ignite,
Guiding us through the darkest night.
Together we forge a silver thread,
In the warmth of words unsaid.

Through laughter shared, joy unfolds,
In every moment, courage holds.
With hands held tight, we journey far,
Finding peace beneath the stars.

Every glance, a silent prayer,
In the stillness, love lays bare.
A bond created, ever strong,
In the echoes where we belong.

In the spaces where souls meet,
Our journeys blend, our hearts beat.
Within the glow of connection's fire,
We rise as one, never tire.

Spirals of Delight

In circles spun with laughter bright,
We dance beneath the soft moonlight.
Every twirl a spark, a cheer,
In this moment, all draws near.

Together we weave a playful game,
In the rhythm, never the same.
With every step, our spirits soar,
In the joy we find, we want more.

A spiral of dreams, twinkling wide,
In this adventure, we take pride.
With open hearts and gleaming eyes,
We chase the whispers of the skies.

Through time and space, our echoes play,
In harmony, we light the way.
Each pulse of joy, a gentle call,
In this infinite loop, we have it all.

With every heartbeat, a story spins,
In laughter and love, where life begins.
Together we dance through day and night,
In spirals of delight, pure and bright.

Shadows of Affection

In corners where the silence dwells,
Shadows whisper, their secrets tell.
Beneath the glow of a fading light,
Love hides softly, out of sight.

With tender gaze, we linger long,
In the stillness, we find our song.
Every breath a gentle sigh,
In the shadows, we learn to fly.

Hesitant hearts in quiet grace,
Finding warmth in an embrace.
Through the tender dusk we roam,
In the shadows, we find our home.

With every moment, time stands still,
In silent vows, we learn to feel.
The depth of love, a hidden glow,
In every shadow, affection flows.

As twilight dances into dawn,
We cherish the ties that linger on.
In shadows cast by love's own hand,
Together forever, we will stand.

Resonant Heartbeats

In the stillness, hearts align,
A rhythm echoes, pure and fine.
Each beat a pulse, a shared embrace,
In harmony, we find our place.

With every thump, our stories blend,
In whispered truths, we comprehend.
Through crowded rooms, our eyes will meet,
In silent songs, our spirits greet.

Resonant murmurs through the air,
In unison, we lay our care.
Every heartbeat sings a song,
In this symphony, we belong.

Moments woven, time stands still,
Together we climb every hill.
In the echoes, love's refrain,
In resonant heartbeats, we remain.

Through trials faced and joys embraced,
Our journey carved, our souls interlaced.
In the tapestry of life we weave,
Resonant heartbeats, we believe.

Circles of Warmth

In the dusk's embrace we linger,
Sharing stories, heartbeats sync.
Fires crackle softly, a singer,
We are tethered, no need to think.

Hands entwined, our laughter sways,
Beneath the stars, in peace we soar.
Time dissolves in endless days,
Our spirits dance, forevermore.

Memories blend, like colors merge,
In this circle, fear fades away.
Together, on this gentle verge,
Love ignites a brighter day.

Whispers travel through the night,
Carried on the crisp, cool air.
Every glance a spark of light,
Promises held with tender care.

As shadows wane and dawn unfolds,
We rise anew, souls intertwined.
In this warmth, our hearts are bold,
Hand in hand, through life we find.

Light of Together

In the quiet glow of evening,
Two souls merging, a soft embrace.
With every glance, our hearts are weaving,
A tapestry, a sacred space.

Laughter twinkles like the stars,
Every moment, joy ignites.
Through the storm and all its scars,
We find solace in shared sights.

Journey onward, step by step,
Guided by the love we share.
In your eyes, my dreams are kept,
A safe haven, pure and rare.

Hand in hand, the path unfurls,
Whatever comes, we face it strong.
In this dance, our spirit swirls,
Finding harmony in our song.

Light each other through the dark,
Beacons bright, we shine anew.
In this life, we leave a mark,
Together, forever true.

Journeying with You

A path unfolds beneath our feet,
Together, we embrace the way.
With every heartbeat, life's a treat,
As memories blossom day by day.

Mountains rise, and valleys fall,
We wander on, side by side.
Through every challenge, we stand tall,
In our bond, we take such pride.

Hand in hand, the world we see,
Painted wild with hues of dreams.
In your gaze, I am set free,
Navigating by love's bright beams.

With whispers soft as morning light,
We map the stars, write our own tale.
In your arms, the world feels right,
Together we shall never fail.

The journey's long, but hearts are true,
Every twist and turn is ours.
In the vastness, just me and you,
As we chase the endless stars.

Colors of Reaction

In the palette of life's embrace,
Every hue tells its own tale.
From vibrant reds to softest grace,
Our emotions stir, never pale.

Joy bursts forth in sunny yellows,
While sorrow shades in hues of blue.
Each feeling flows like gentle meadows,
In this canvas, I find you.

Greens of hope bloom wide and free,
As dreams take flight on wings of gold.
In every splash, we paint the sea,
Our bright stories forever bold.

Colors collide, create what's new,
Each brushstroke, a moment shared.
In this masterpiece, just us two,
With love's design, we are prepared.

As twilight deepens, shadows blend,
The spectrum fades to a gentle night.
Yet in my heart, the colors send,
A promise that we'll chase the light.

Circles of Affection

In gentle whispers, bonds arise,
Drawing hearts beneath the skies.
A laughter shared, pure and bright,
In circles woven, love takes flight.

Hands held tight through storms and calm,
Each tender touch, a healing balm.
We dance in time, our spirits free,
In circles of affection, you and me.

The warmth of friendship, a glowing light,
Guiding us through the dark of night.
Every memory etched in gold,
In treasured tales, our love unfolds.

Seasons change, but roots run deep,
In trust and care, our secrets keep.
With open hearts, we share our dreams,
In circles of affection, love redeems.

So let us gather, hand in hand,
In this sacred, joyful band.
Together we'll rise, together we'll grow,
In endless circles, love will flow.

Flowing Streams of Understanding

Beneath the surface, currents flow,
Revealing truths we long to know.
With every drop, a story sings,
In flowing streams, our heart takes wings.

In quiet moments, thoughts aligned,
With gentle hearts, the ties we find.
We listen close, in silence shared,
In flowing streams, our souls are bared.

Through twists and turns, we learn of grace,
Embracing each unique embrace.
A dance of minds, forever true,
In flowing streams, I flow with you.

Like rivers merge, our paths entwine,
In sacred trust, your heart is mine.
With every whisper, healing starts,
In flowing streams, we share our hearts.

Together we navigate the tide,
In understanding, side by side.
The wisdom gained, a cherished gift,
In flowing streams, our spirits lift.

Unspoken Affinities

In quiet corners, feelings grow,
A glance exchanged, no need to show.
Like shadows dancing in the light,
In unspoken affinities, we unite.

Words unneeded, hearts can feel,
Emotions deep and truly real.
In silent echoes, truths reside,
In unspoken affinities, side by side.

The comfort found in simple gaze,
A shared heartbeat, a subtle praise.
Through every moment, we connect,
In unspoken affinities, respect.

Laughter lingers upon the air,
In secret worlds, we boldly dare.
Together weaving dreams anew,
In unspoken affinities, me and you.

So let us cherish, day by day,
This hidden bond, this gentle play.
With every heartbeat, understand,
In unspoken affinities, take my hand.

Celestial Harmonies

Underneath the vast expanse,
We find our place in cosmic dance.
Stars align in splendid grace,
In celestial harmonies, we embrace.

The moonlight whispers soft and cool,
Guiding us like an ancient rule.
With every twinkle, hopes arise,
In celestial harmonies, love lies.

Galaxies spin, a waltz divine,
In this universe, your heart is mine.
A symphony of light and sound,
In celestial harmonies, we're found.

Through comets' tails and meteor showers,
We trace our dreams in midnight hours.
With every pulse, our spirits soar,
In celestial harmonies, forevermore.

So take my hand beneath the night,
Together we'll reach celestial light.
In this grand tapestry, we belong,
In celestial harmonies, our love's song.

Portrait of Togetherness

In laughter and in quiet grace,
We find a warm embracing space.
A canvas filled with colors bright,
Together we create our light.

Through trials faced, we stand as one,
A shared journey just begun.
With every heartbeat, every sigh,
We're tied beneath the endless sky.

In whispered dreams and softest tunes,
We dance beneath the silver moons.
Through storms that rage and winds that call,
Hand in hand, we shall not fall.

The threads of life weave strong and true,
As you and I, we paint anew.
A masterpiece of love and care,
A bond no shadow can impair.

So here we stand, our hearts aligned,
In this portrait, love defined.
Together, through the years we'll grow,
In every moment, let it show.

Whirlwind of Emotions

A storm brews deep within my chest,
With waves of doubt and fleeting rest.
Passions rise like tides at sea,
Pulling me where I long to be.

Joy and sorrow intertwine,
A dance of fate, a twisted vine.
Each heartbeat echoes through the void,
A symphony of feelings, enjoyed.

Love ignites like sparks in the night,
While fear lingers, blurring the light.
Moments of bliss, then shadows creep,
In this whirlwind, I find no sleep.

Hope like a feather floats on air,
Yet doubt weighs heavy, hard to bear.
Through every twist and every turn,
I seek the peace for which I yearn.

But in this chaos, I find my way,
Emotions guide me day by day.
In every gust, a lesson learned,
In this whirlwind, my heart has burned.

Symphony of Shared Dreams

In the hush of evening's glow,
We weave our dreams, let passions flow.
Notes of hope dance on the breeze,
In harmony, we find our ease.

With every vision, hand in hand,
Together we will make our stand.
A melody that lifts us high,
With every heartbeat, we touch the sky.

Through valleys deep and mountains tall,
Our symphony of dreams enthralls.
In whispered songs and laughter bright,
We chase the stars, igniting light.

In the tapestry of night we trace,
The dreams we've held in sweet embrace.
With every note, our spirits sing,
In this moment, we are everything.

So let us gather, near and far,
In the presence of the evening star.
For every dream, together we'll find,
A timeless echo, soul entwined.

Unity's Silent Song

In quiet moments, we are one,
Beneath the gaze of setting sun.
A gentle peace flows through the air,
In silence, we become a prayer.

No words are needed, just the sigh,
Of hearts in rhythm, you and I.
In every glance, a story told,
A bond that never will grow old.

With unspoken hopes, we intertwine,
A melody soft, sweet, and divine.
In every heartbeat, an embrace,
In unity, we find our place.

Through shadows cast and light that beams,
We dance together in our dreams.
No louder sound than love can sing,
In silence, unity takes wing.

So here we stand, hand in hand,
In the stillness of this land.
For in the silence, love is strong,
Together, we create a song.

Symphony of Emotions

In whispers soft, the heart confides,
A melody where pain abides.
Joy dances lightly on the breeze,
While sorrow sinks like autumn leaves.

Each note a tale, each chord a theme,
In twilight's glow, we chase a dream.
Love crescendos, rising high,
While fears subsist, yet never die.

Harmony of laughter, tears below,
In shadows cast, the light will grow.
The symphony entwines our souls,
Through every rise and whispered tolls.

Together in this vivid sound,
Our voices meld, forever bound.
An opus rich, of life defined,
In music's grasp, our hearts aligned.

Through every fall, and every flight,
The symphony ignites the night.
In every heartbeat, every sigh,
Our song will live, it will not die.

Heartbeats in Unison

Two souls entwined in tender grace,
With every heartbeat, find their place.
Rhythms pulse beneath the skin,
In silent vows, our love begins.

Moments shared, each laugh, each tear,
Echoes of dreams, drawing near.
In shadowed corners, light will seep,
As hand in hand, our secrets keep.

The quiet strength, a sacred bond,
In storms we weather, we respond.
With hearts in sync, we rise and fall,
Together strong, we'll brave it all.

Beneath the stars, our dreams will soar,
In every heartbeat, we'll explore.
A symphony that's ours to claim,
With every beat, we play the game.

Forever bound, like whispering winds,
In unison, our love begins.
With every thrum, we sing our song,
In harmony, where we belong.

Reflected Warmth

In morning light, your smile gleams,
A tranquil balm, like gentle dreams.
With every glance, I feel the spark,
A tender warmth that lights the dark.

The sunlit glow upon your face,
Each moment shared, a warm embrace.
Reflections dance on every wave,
In this warm light, together brave.

Through seasons change, as shadows fall,
Your laughter brightens, love through all.
In mirrored moments, time suspends,
In every breath, our hearts extend.

With every step, we journey through,
The warmth in you, the light so true.
In silent whispers, dreams will spark,
While reflected love ignites the dark.

In twilight's glow, our shadows blend,
A cherished warmth that will not end.
Together, here, our hearts reside,
In mirrored warmth, we shall abide.

Celestial Embrace

Underneath the cosmic eye,
Two hearts entwined, without a sigh.
In starlit whispers, dreams align,
With every breath, your soul is mine.

Galaxies spin, the night unfolds,
A dance of light, a tale retold.
In moonlit paths, our spirits glide,
With every moment, love's our guide.

The universe sings a timeless tune,
As constellations draw us close, in bloom.
In this vastness, we find our place,
A sacred hour, a warm embrace.

Through cosmic tides, we journey forth,
In every star, we find our worth.
Celestial bodies, hand in hand,
Together wandering, fate so grand.

In stellar dreams, we lose our fears,
With every heartbeat, chase the years.
In this embrace, our spirits soar,
Forever wrapped in love's encore.

Palette of Pulses

Colors dance on canvas bright,
Emotions swirl, a vivid sight.
Brush strokes whisper tales untold,
In hues of warmth, and shadows bold.

A heartbeat thumps in shades of blue,
Secret dreams in every hue.
Crimson laughter fills the air,
Every pulse, a vibrant flare.

Golden rays of morning sun,
Bring to light what hearts have spun.
Each layer deep, a story's thread,
A palette rich, where souls are fed.

Within the frame, we find our place,
Unity in colors' grace.
A swirling blend that cannot part,
Each tone, a beat within the heart.

In silence speaks the visual song,
Echoes where we all belong.
In every stroke, a pulse alive,
Art, the breath in which we thrive.

Caress of Kindred Spirits

In whispers soft, our souls entwined,
A gentle touch where hearts aligned.
Through laughter shared and tears we shed,
In warmth and light, our paths are led.

Beneath the stars, we chase the night,
Each glance, a spark, a guiding light.
In every moment, truth we seek,
In silence deep, both strong and meek.

With every breath, connection grows,
A harmony that ebbs and flows.
Together we rise, together we fall,
In love's embrace, we have it all.

The dance of spirits, intertwined,
In every heartbeat, love defined.
Through storms and calm, forever near,
In every laugh, in every tear.

Through winding paths, our journey flows,
In kindness shared, true beauty glows.
With every thread, we weave our fate,
In this caress, we celebrate.

Interwoven Desires

In candlelight, we share our dreams,
Whispers soft, like flowing streams.
Two hearts entwined, a dance so sweet,
In each embrace, our worlds complete.

With every glance, a spark ignites,
In the silence, passion bites.
Desires bloom like flowers rare,
In fragrant air, we lay our care.

Fingers trace what words can't say,
In night's embrace, we drift away.
With gentle sighs, our souls collide,
In woven moments, worlds abide.

Each heartbeat hums a secret tune,
Underneath the glowing moon.
In twilight's hold, our futures blend,
In this dance, we have no end.

The tapestry of hearts we weave,
In every touch, we learn to believe.
Desires mixed, a vivid thread,
In this embrace, our spirits fed.

Celestial Cadence

Stars shimmer bright in endless night,
A cosmic dance, a wondrous sight.
In orbits vast, our hopes align,
In stellar glow, our dreams combine.

The moonlight bathes our whispered prayers,
In cosmic winds, our spirit dares.
With every breath, the universe sighs,
In harmonic waves, our essence flies.

Galaxies cradle our hearts' embrace,
In celestial realms, we find our place.
Shooting stars, our wishes cast,
In timeless rhythm, we hold fast.

The melody of night, divine,
In every heartbeat, love's design.
Under the sky, we dance as one,
In celestial cadence, we run.

Forever held in cosmic grace,
In the fabric of time, we trace.
With stardust dreams and spirits free,
In this vast realm, we'll always be.

Interlaced Journeys

In shadows deep, we find our way,
Through tangled paths, where whispers sway,
With every step, our spirits guide,
Together we move, side by side.

The world unfolds in hues so bright,
With laughter shared, we chase the light,
In every turn, a lesson learned,
In every spark, our passions burned.

Moments fleeting, yet they hold,
Stories woven, warm and bold,
With hands entwined, we leave our mark,
As stars above ignite the dark.

Through valleys low, and mountains high,
We'll seek the truth that never dies,
In whispered dreams, we dare to soar,
Each journey lived, we yearn for more.

So take my hand, let's venture forth,
In every heartbeat, treasure worth,
Together we'll write our own refrain,
Interlaced, through joy and pain.

Reflections of Intimacy

In quiet moments, hearts align,
Gentle gazes, soft and fine,
Secrets shared in the silence deep,
Promises made in whispers, we keep.

With every touch, a story told,
In warmth of presence, love unfolds,
A dance of souls, entwined as one,
Under the gaze of the golden sun.

Together we flourish, through thick and thin,
In storms of life, we find our kin,
With laughter and tears, the fabric we weave,
In the tapestry of trust, we believe.

As shadows pass, and days grow long,
In each heartbeat, we find our song,
In the gentle rhythm, hearts will sway,
In reflections of love, we choose to stay.

Through time's embrace, we'll never part,
In every moment, you fill my heart,
With every breath, our spirits entwined,
In the dance of intimacy, love defined.

Beneath the Same Stars

Under velvet skies, dreams take flight,
Whispers of hope in the still of night,
Every twinkle tells a tale,
Of love and fate, we shall not fail.

With every glance upon the sky,
We feel the pull, the how and why,
Connected deeply, though far apart,
Beneath the same stars, beats one heart.

In constellations, our stories blend,
In cosmic dance, our spirits mend,
As moons rise high, and shadows shift,
In this shared space, our souls uplift.

Through the gentle sway of time and tide,
In every challenge, love is our guide,
In the silence vast, we find our grace,
Beneath the same stars, our sacred place.

As night fades, and dawn breaks clear,
In every heartbeat, I feel you near,
For distance means not what love imparts,
As we journey on, with open hearts.

Unbroken Circles

In the cycle of life, we find our way,
With every season, a brand-new day,
In laughter shared, and tears we know,
Together we dance, as rivers flow.

From beginnings soft to endings sweet,
In the journey's heart, our spirits meet,
Through twists and turns, we remain strong,
In the unbroken circle, we belong.

In moments fleeting, we capture time,
In rhythms shared, our hearts in rhyme,
With kindness shown, in deeds and words,
In the circle of trust, love is heard.

Through every trial, and each delight,
In the bond we hold, there shines a light,
With open arms, we embrace the flow,
In unbroken circles, our love will grow.

As chapters close, new ones turn,
In every lesson, our hearts will learn,
In the simplest joys and trials faced,
In unbroken circles, we find our place.

Vibrating with Affinity

In whispers soft, our spirits hum,
A dance of light, where hearts are one.
Each laughter shared, a sacred vow,
Together we bloom, here and now.

In twilight's glow, our secrets weave,
A tapestry rich, in love we believe.
With every spark, our essence stirs,
Connected souls, as time gently blurs.

The rhythm beats, a timeless song,
In every glance, we both belong.
Through storms we share, both joy and pain,
In unity's arms, we break every chain.

With open hearts, we journey far,
Guided always by our brightest star.
Through valleys deep and mountains high,
In harmony, we learn to fly.

So here we stand, as one we rise,
With every breath, we touch the skies.
Vibrating strong, in sync we find,
Our souls forever intertwined.

In Tune with Tomorrow

Awake, the dawn begins to glow,
Brush strokes of light on fields below.
With hopes aglow, we chase the day,
In dreams of gold, we'll find our way.

A melody plays on the gentle breeze,
In whispers soft, it puts us at ease.
Each note a promise, a future bright,
Together we step, into the light.

With every moment, the world ignites,
In laughter shared, we reach new heights.
With hearts aligned, we face each storm,
A bond unbroken, forever warm.

The paths we tread may twist and bend,
In every turn, our spirits mend.
With every challenge, we learn to soar,
In tune with tomorrow, forevermore.

So take my hand, as we ignite,
A symphony born from day and night.
With love as our guide, we'll make our claim,
In tune with tomorrow, we'll stake our name.

Across the Boundaries

Beyond the walls, where shadows fade,
We seek the dreams that love has made.
With open hearts and fearless eyes,
We break the chains, we cut the ties.

Through distant lands, our voices soar,
A bridge of hope, forevermore.
With every step, we forge the path,
In unity's arms, we find our math.

The stars above, a guiding light,
In darkness deep, they shine so bright.
Across the boundaries we now roam,
In every heart, we find our home.

With gentle hands, we weave our fate,
A tapestry rich, we celebrate.
Together we rise, hands intertwined,
Across the boundaries, our souls aligned.

So let us dance, unbound by fear,
With hearts ablaze, we draw near.
In every heartbeat, a promise found,
Across the boundaries, we are unbound.

Hearth of Completeness

In the warm glow of the hearth, we sit,
Stories unfold, as embers emit.
Around this fire, our spirits share,
A haven safe, where love is rare.

With every laugh, the shadows fade,
In brightness found, our fears are laid.
Through gentle whispers, dreams take flight,
In the hearth's embrace, we own the night.

The warmth surrounds, like tender grace,
In this sacred space, we find our place.
With hands held tight, we face the storm,
In the hearth of completeness, we stay warm.

With every heartbeat, our stories blend,
A circle of trust, where souls transcend.
In laughter's echo, we hold what's true,
In the hearth of completeness, it's me and you.

So gather 'round, the night is young,
In the dance of voices, our song is sung.
With hearts aglow, we find our peace,
At the hearth of completeness, love will increase.

Bonds Beyond Words

In silent spaces, we find our way,
Shared glances say what words can't convey.
Through laughter and tears, we hold tight,
Together we shine, like stars in the night.

A touch, a smile, a knowing gaze,
In simple moments, our hearts we raise.
No need for speech, our spirits entwined,
In the warmth of each other, true love defined.

Through trials faced and triumphs won,
Our connection deepens, two become one.
In every silence, our souls converse,
A bond unbroken, in universe.

With every heartbeat, stories unfold,
In every embrace, a tale retold.
The echoes of laughter, the shadows of pain,
In this journey together, all joys remain.

Beyond the noise, in this sacred space,
Our hearts united, we perfectly grace.
For in each moment, a truth we hold,
Bonds beyond words, a love that's bold.

Ode to Companionship

Hand in hand, through thick and thin,
In the warmth of your smile, I feel the win.
With every step on this lifelong road,
Together we lighten the burdens bestowed.

In whispers shared, and dreams we dare,
Your laughter dances in the crisp air.
In every challenge, a shared embrace,
With you beside me, I find my place.

Through sunsets painted in hues so bright,
In your company, the world feels right.
A treasure cherished, a journey begun,
In our togetherness, we've already won.

From quiet talks to wild adventures,
In every moment, our hearts are ventures.
The tales we weave, the memories spun,
An ode to companionship, forever one.

With every heartbeat, our lives align,
In each other's presence, we brightly shine.
For in this union, a promise we weave,
An enduring bond, together we believe.

Unity in Diversity

In different colors, we paint the sky,
With varied voices, our spirits fly.
In harmony, we seek to understand,
A tapestry woven, hand in hand.

Through storms of doubt and winds of change,
Our differences bloom, beautifully strange.
In every culture, a story unfolds,
In each of our hearts, a treasure of gold.

From mountains high to valleys low,
In diversity's embrace, love does grow.
With open minds and giving hearts,
We create a world where no one departs.

Together we dance to a vibrant tune,
Under the glow of a welcoming moon.
In unity's cradle, strength we find,
In every heartbeat, all are aligned.

So let us gather, in joy and in peace,
In this grand mosaic, where love won't cease.
For in our differences, the truth is revealed,
In unity, our hearts are healed.

Resonating Heartbeats

With every pulse, a rhythm shared,
In the quiet moments, we find we're paired.
Through gentle whispers and breaths so near,
In the echoing stillness, our hearts appear.

Stars above mirror the spark below,
In the dance of life, our energies flow.
In the space between breaths, a story unfolds,
With pulsating life, our connection holds.

From laughter's cadence to silence profound,
In resonating heartbeats, our love is found.
Every thump tells tales of joy and sorrow,
In unity, we shape each tomorrow.

With hands entwined, we leap and soar,
In this journey of chaos, we crave for more.
Through trials weathered and moments bright,
Our heartbeats align in stunning light.

In every heartbeat, a promise is cast,
In this shared life, we've built to last.
For through the rhythms that life imparts,
Resonating heartbeats, two loving hearts.

Embracing Echoes

In shadows soft, I hear your call,
A whisper lingers, echoing all.
Through twilight's veil, our spirits roam,
In the silence, I find my home.

The stars align, their glow is near,
Each flicker whispers, 'I am here.'
With every heartbeat, we intertwine,
In this dance of love, so divine.

Through valleys low and mountains high,
Our dreams take flight beneath the sky.
Together, side by side we stand,
In the embrace of fate's sweet hand.

The world may fade, its colors blur,
Yet in your gaze, my heart will stir.
With every echo, a story unfolds,
In timeless moments, our truth behold.

So let us wander, hand in hand,
In this dreamscape, forever planned.
With every breath, our love's refrain,
In echoes soft, we will remain.

Whirl of Togetherness

In circles spun, we dance through night,
With laughter shared, pure delight.
Two souls entwined in rhythm's grace,
We find our joy in this embrace.

Amidst the whirl, the world can fade,
A tapestry of dreams we've made.
As time slows down, we lose the chase,
In every glance, a warm embrace.

Let worries drift like leaves in air,
In this safe space, we have no care.
With every twirl, two hearts align,
In the whirl of love, we brightly shine.

The music swells, our spirits soar,
In perfect sync, we crave for more.
Together lost, forever found,
In love's sweet whirl, our hearts resound.

So hold me close, don't let me go,
In this bright dance, we'll always glow.
Through every step, our spirits blend,
In this great whirl, our love won't end.

Raindrops on Heartstrings

Gentle whispers fall from above,
Each drop a note, a song of love.
They tap and dance on windowpanes,
In their rhythm, I hear your name.

A soothing balm on weary days,
Raindrops play soft, in nature's ways.
They weave through branches, trails of grace,
Connecting hearts in every place.

Through puddles deep, our dreams take flight,
In every splash, a glimpse of light.
With heartstrings tinged by silver rain,
We find our peace amidst the pain.

Each raindrop tells a tale of hope,
In downpour's dance, we learn to cope.
With every pulse, our love remains,
In melody of soft refrains.

So let it rain, let shadows fall,
In every drop, I hear your call.
Together bound, through storms we sing,
In raindrops' grace, our hearts take wing.

Love's Gentle Chime

In morning light, your laughter rings,
A melody that softly clings.
With every word, a tender rhyme,
Echoing sweetly, love's gentle chime.

Through quiet nights, we share our dreams,
In whispered thoughts, the starlight beams.
We weave a story, page by page,
In love's embrace, we find our stage.

As seasons change, our hearts will grow,
With every challenge, love will flow.
Hand in hand, we face the climb,
Together strong, love's endless prime.

With every heartbeat, a song unfolds,
The warmth of love, a treasure holds.
In sunlight's glow and autumn's time,
We dance in rhythm, love's gentle chime.

So through the years, our spirits soar,
In every moment, we love more.
With joyful hearts, we stand in line,
For life's sweet journey, love will shine.

Resonance of Love's Embrace

In hush of night, hearts intertwine,
Soft whispers echo, sweet and divine.
Hands gently clasp beneath the stars,
A dance of souls, erasing the scars.

Time stands still in this sacred space,
Wrapped in warmth of love's embrace.
Every heartbeat speaks a tale,
In silent vows, we will not fail.

Dreams are painted on twilight's glow,
In the garden where wildflowers grow.
With every glance, a spark ignites,
Turning darkness into soft light.

Threads of fate in tender weave,
Together in joy, we believe.
Each moment lingers, rich and pure,
In love's embrace, we find our cure.

Through storms that rage and winds that sigh,
Together we soar, we learn to fly.
In the resonance, our hearts combine,
An eternal rhythm, forever entwined.

Interlude of Serendipity

Amidst the chaos, a glance we share,
A fleeting moment in the air.
Paths crossing where fate has cried,
In this interlude, we confide.

With laughter's echo, our spirits rise,
In unexpected joy, no disguise.
A gentle touch, a smile exchanged,
In this serendipity, lives rearranged.

Fingers dance on a table's edge,
Words unspoken form a pledge.
When stars align, we chase the dawn,
In this sweet pause, all fears are gone.

Every heartbeat tells us to stay,
In the magic of this day.
Moments weave a shining thread,
In this tapestry of love, we're led.

Let time linger, let the music play,
In serendipity, we drift away.
A breathless sigh, a cherished chance,
In the dance of souls, we find romance.

Love's Gentle Cadence

Softly spoken, words like rain,
Each syllable a sweet refrain.
In tender tones, our secrets blend,
In love's cadence, we transcend.

Heartbeat echoes, a steady drum,
In the rhythm, we become one.
As seasons change, we hold on tight,
In love's cadence, there's pure light.

Moments linger, a gentle sway,
In quiet whispers, come what may.
With every breath, we find our way,
In love's soft dance, forever stay.

Eyes that sparkle, dreams take flight,
Under the stars, we ignite.
Love's melody, a song so true,
In every note, I find you.

Through the valleys, we will tread,
In love's cadence, our fears shed.
Together always, hearts ablaze,
In this gentle love, we forever gaze.

Celestial Confluence

In cosmic dance, our souls align,
Under the moon, in space divine.
Stars enchant in the night so bright,
In celestial confluence, pure delight.

Galaxies whisper, a timeless song,
In this union, where we belong.
With every beat, the heavens sigh,
A tapestry woven in the sky.

In the nebula's glow, we ignite,
Two constellations, burning bright.
Paths entwined in a cosmic flow,
In the vastness, our love will grow.

As comets trail through inked abyss,
Every touch becomes a kiss.
We navigate the stars above,
In celestial confluence, we find love.

So let the universe sing our song,
In this dance, where we belong.
With every heartbeat, worlds collide,
In love's embrace, we will abide.

Echoes of Souls Entwined

In shadows deep, we find our grace,
Whispers soft, a timeless embrace.
Hearts aligned, two paths collide,
In the echo of love, we confide.

Through twilight's glow, our spirits soar,
Each heartbeat sounds, a sacred roar.
Bound by dreams, we rise and fall,
In the silence, we hear the call.

With every star, a tale unfolds,
In radiant hues, our story's told.
Together we chase the night so bright,
In the dance of fate, we find our light.

Serenade of Kindred Spirits

In gentle tones, our voices blend,
A symphony that has no end.
Through laughter sweet and sorrows deep,
Kindred hearts, a promise we keep.

Beneath the moon, where dreams ignite,
We share our stories, pure delight.
In the stillness, secrets flow,
With every sigh, our spirits glow.

In every glance, a spark is found,
A rhythm thrums, a sacred sound.
Together we sail, the tides of time,
In the love we share, a perfect rhyme.

Dance of Intertwined Rhythms

In the twilight haze, our bodies sway,
With every beat, we drift away.
A melody shared, a heartbeat's song,
In this dance of life, we both belong.

Fingers entwined, we move as one,
Under the gaze of the setting sun.
With every turn, the world dissolves,
In this embrace, our hearts evolve.

With laughter's pulse and passion's fire,
We rise and fall—our souls conspire.
In the rhythm of dusk, we find our way,
In every step, love's sweet ballet.

Merging Melodies

In quiet hush, our dreams unite,
As day meets dusk in hues of light.
A song of hope, a harmony's thread,
In every note, our hearts are led.

Together we weave the fabric of fate,
In whispered tones, we celebrate.
With every chord, a bond defined,
In the music shared, our souls aligned.

Through laughter's rise and sorrow's fall,
In every moment, we give our all.
In the dance of time, we find our voice,
In the merging of melodies, we rejoice.

Dance of Resonance

In shadows where the echoes play,
Two spirits sway in twilight's grace.
Every heartbeat starts to fray,
In rhythm's arms, they find their place.

The moonlight drapes a silver veil,
As whispers dance upon the breeze.
In unity, they tell a tale,
A song of love that never flees.

With every step, their hopes ignite,
In circles drawn by fate's own hands.
Together shining, pure and bright,
They spin the magic that expands.

Through laughter shared and silent tears,
The music flows like flowing streams.
They face the world, cast aside fears,
In this embrace, they share their dreams.

As dawn breaks in a soft caress,
Their dance goes on in endless night.
In every move, a sweet confess,
They twirl in love, a boundless flight.

Tapestry of Togetherness

Threads of laughter weave in time,
Each color brightens shadows cast.
In every stitch, a beat, a rhyme,
A bond that holds us ever fast.

In gatherings, our stories blend,
Creating patterns, bold and new.
With every heart, a love to send,
In unity, we'll share our hue.

The weaver's hands in motion free,
Crafting moments filled with light.
In tangled fates, we're meant to be,
Together shining through the night.

With every knot, a memory,
An echo of the days gone by.
In threads of gold, we find our key,
To unlock dreams that reach the sky.

As seasons change, the fabric grows,
A masterpiece of joy and tears.
In every fold, our journey shows,
A tapestry to last for years.

Shared Dreams Aflutter

In twilight's soft and tender glow,
Two souls unite, the stars align.
With whispered hopes, their spirits flow,
In every heartbeat, love's design.

A canvas spread, both wide and vast,
They paint their dreams in shades of night.
Each vision blooms, a spell is cast,
Their laughter sparkles, pure delight.

Through gentle winds, their wishes soar,
On wings of fate, they take their flight.
Hand in hand, they seek for more,
In every pulse, the world feels right.

In quiet spaces, hearts entwined,
They share the stories yet untold.
In unity, their dreams combined,
A narrative of love unfolds.

With every dawn, their hopes revive,
A tapestry of fancies spun.
Together, through the years, they thrive,
In shared dreams, their journey's won.

Unity in Diversity

In gardens bright where blossoms sway,
Each petal tells a tale unique.
In colors bold, they find their way,
Together strong, and none too weak.

From distant lands, we gather close,
In harmony, our voices rise.
A chorus loud, each note, a dose,
Of strength divine, under the skies.

Through trials faced and struggles met,
We weave a fabric vast and true.
In bonds of love, no room for regret,
In every heart, a shared view.

With hands clasped tight, our dreams will soar,
Across the lands, we'll break the mold.
In unity, we will explore,
A future bright, together bold.

As stars above, our souls connect,
In every heart, a different beat.
In this embrace, we find respect,
United, strong, and truly sweet.

Heartfelt Intermission

In the soft glow of twilight's wrap,
Whispers of love begin to tap.
Moments linger, suspended in time,
Hearts beat gently, in sweet rhyme.

Silence dances in the air,
Each breath shared, a tender care.
Dreams unfold like petals wide,
In this space, our souls abide.

Echoes linger, a warm embrace,
In every smile, we find our place.
Time stands still, a sacred pause,
In this intermission, love draws.

Memories drift on softest breeze,
Gentle thoughts that aim to please.
We share the weight of fleeting days,
In every moment, love conveys.

As shadows stretch and night descends,
We find the peace that love extends.
Heartfelt intermission, serene and bright,
In our connection, we find light.

Vibrations of Kindness

With every smile, a seed we sow,
In gentle hearts, kindness will grow.
Together we weave a fabric strong,
In unity's chorus, we all belong.

A touch of grace in every hand,
In understanding, we firmly stand.
Ripples spread from acts so small,
Vibrations of kindness embrace us all.

Through caring words, we ignite the flame,
Of compassion's light, forever the same.
In the rhythms of hearts that align,
Kindness echoes, divine and fine.

Let laughter burst and joy expand,
In the warmth of love, we make our stand.
Together we find harmony's song,
In vibrations of kindness, we grow strong.

Each gesture softens the world's harsh gaze,
In simple acts, love's warm blaze.
Together we rise, with spirits intertwined,
In every heartbeat, kindness defined.

Synchronicity of Souls

In quiet moments, fate unfolds,
Tales of two souls, silently told.
Paths intertwine like threads of fate,
In the cosmic dance, we resonate.

A glance exchanged, a spark ignites,
Across the distance, our spirits unite.
In serendipity's graceful flow,
We find the signs that gently glow.

The universe sings in perfect tone,
In every heartbeat, we're never alone.
Every coincidence, a gentle pull,
In synchronicity, our hearts are full.

Whispers from dreams echo clear,
Guiding us near, dispelling fear.
With every step, we bravely tread,
In this journey, our souls are led.

Together we seek, in harmony's embrace,
In the tapestry of love, we find our place.
For in each moment, our spirits entwine,
In the synchronicity of souls, we shine.

Flicker of Connection

In the crowded room, a glance was shared,
A fleeting moment, yet deeply cared.
Lights may dim, and shadows may fall,
But that flicker remains, connecting us all.

Words unspoken, eyes that meet,
In that silence, our hearts repeat.
The world fades, just you and I,
In the flickering glow, we can't deny.

A bridge built on trust and truth,
In every moment, the joy of youth.
We dance between hopes and dreams,
In this connection, our spirit beams.

As whispers grow into heartfelt calls,
Every heartbeat in rhythm enthralls.
In the tapestry woven with light,
A flicker ignites, a bond ignites.

Though time may shift, and paths may stray,
That flicker of connection will find a way.
In every memory, it brightly glows,
A timeless bond, wherever life goes.

Milton Keynes UK
Ingram Content Group UK Ltd.
UKHW020724071124
450744UK00023B/127

9 789916 869208